HEY! HO! LET'S GO!

SIDE B

8. Loudmouth
9. Havana Affair
10. Listen to My Heart
11. 53rd & 3rd
12. Let's Dance
13. I Don't Wanna
    Walk Around with You
14. Today Your Love,
    Tomorrow the World

RAMONES

The Unauthorized Biography

Written by Soledad Romero Mariño
Illustrated by Joe Padilla

sourcebooks
eXplore

1974 – NEW YORK (FOREST HILLS, QUEENS)

FORMATION OF THE BAND

OFFICIAL DEBUT AND FIRST CONCERT

CONCERT AT ICONIC CBGB

1974

March 30, 1974

August 16, 1974

1976 – LONDON (ROUNDHOUSE, CAMDEN TOWN)

RECORDING THE FIRST ALBUM

January–February 1976

FIRST ALBUM IS RELEASED

April 23, 1976

TRIP TO EUROPE AND SUCCESS IN LONDON

July 1976

FOUR FRIENDS IN THE NEIGHBORHOOD

This story begins in the early seventies, in Queens, New York City, where people from many different countries and ethnic groups called home. It was a colorful and lively neighborhood, full of hope and opportunity.

It was in that neighborhood that four teenagers—Joey, Johnny, Tommy, and Dee Dee—met and shared their passion for music.

A BAND CALLED THE RAMONES

The people in the neighborhood eyed the four boys skeptically—the guys were hopeless with girls and terrible in school. They didn't have many friends, and spent most of their time in Joey's mom's art gallery listening to rock records.

One day, Johnny and Dee Dee showed up with second-hand guitars and the four friends decided to form a band called the Ramones.

Being called "the Ramones" was Tommy's idea—it came from "Paul Ramone," the fake name that musician Paul McCartney of the Beatles used to check into hotels in order to avoid harassment from fans.

From that day, every member of the band would adopt the surname "Ramone."

REHEARSAL

They had all previously belonged to a neighborhood band, but none of them could play an instrument very well. The road wouldn't be easy, but they were all eager to create something authentic as the Ramones.

The boys tried several different lineups until they found the formula that would make them legends:

Joey Ramone as the voice, Johnny Ramone on guitar, Dee Dee Ramone on bass, and Tommy Ramone on drums.

JOEY RAMONE
(JEFFREY ROSS HYMANN)

Joey Ramone was born in New York and grew up with his mother, who inspired him in the world of art and music. He was a shy and unique boy, extremely thin, six-and-a-half feet tall, and always hid his eyes behind sunglasses, usually with red lenses.

Joey started out on drums, but quickly became the lead singer of the band. He performed with his long legs stuck firmly to the stage, his body tilting, and his hands clutching the microphone, wailing and shouting as if there were no tomorrow. He also composed many of the band's songs.

JOHNNY RAMONE
(JOHN WILLIAM CUMMINGS)

Undoubtedly the rowdiest member of the group, Johnny Ramone was a teenager who was angry with life. His parents sent him to military school, hoping that a firm hand could tame the beast inside him, but soon Johnny returned to the neighborhood just as rebellious as before.

Johnny was a powerful guitarist, and went out on stage knowing that he and his band were the best. He would slam defiant chords at full speed on the Mosrite guitar strapped around his shoulder.

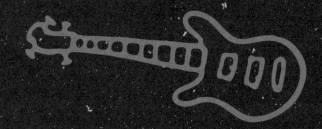

DEE DEE RAMONE
(DOUGLAS GLENN COLVIN)

Dee Dee Ramone was born in the United States, but spent his childhood with his family in Germany. He returned to America as a teenager.

Dee Dee was a very sensitive boy who lived in a universe of total fantasy. He was a poet who saw music as an escape. To earn money when the band first formed, he wandered through the streets of New York looking for odd jobs.

In addition to writing a large part of the Ramones repertoire and being in charge of the bass, he was the one who marked the beginning of each song with the iconic cry of "1, 2, 3, 4!" He also sang backup to Joey.

TOMMY RAMONE
(THOMAS ERDELTI)

Tommy Ramone was born in Hungary. When he was a young boy, he and his family emigrated to the United States to escape the growing violence in Hungary.

He had a better understanding of the music world than his bandmates. It was he who most insisted on putting a band together, and who secured their rehearsal space and first concerts.

Tommy wrote some of the songs and took over on the drums when Joey became the lead singer. He was the rhythm and the sanity of the group as they wandered the alleys of rock and punk.

FIRST CONCERT

After practicing for a few weeks, the Ramones made their first official appearance as a band in a rehearsal hall. The concert was only attended by some friends of theirs—there were no more than thirty people in the room.

The guys went on stage without having done their homework—they didn't sing their own songs and were unable to keep up with the rhythms they started. In fact, the characteristic "1, 2, 3, 4" that Dee Dee opened the songs with was the only way they could all start at the same time. Uncoordinated and clumsy with their instruments, their first concert was a forgettable one.

From that concert on, after several fights and a lot of practice and work, they improved their playing and even started writing their own songs.

DEBUT AT CBGB

A few months later, the Ramones managed to book a concert at CBGB, a cramped, grungy music club. It was a lively venue, popular among artists and moderns, and was one of the coolest places in New York City.

That night, the room held about three hundred people. The restless audience watched as the four gangly, hairy guys played at full volume. A good portion of the spectators left the club covering their ears from the noise. Others, however, understood that this band was playing rock as it should be played—with rawness, strength, and intensity. The band got invited back and played at CBGB every week.

The Ramones were anti-heroes with the desire to show the world what they could do, with or without the audience's applause.

THE RAMONES: THE HYMN OF A TRIBE

The Ramones spoke and dressed as other young people on the streets did, and for this reason they became representatives of a tribe and a generation.

They wore black leather jackets, high-top sneakers, T-shirts, and tattered pants with holes in them. They demonstrated that it wasn't necessary to have a typical luxurious image to play rock.

The Ramones' image became the day-to-day symbol of the punk revolution.

RECORDING THE FIRST ALBUM

For months, the Ramones played in theaters and venues in the Big Apple, gaining confidence and strength with each concert.

Rock magazines began to write about them, and one day their music reached the ears of the owner of a small label: Sire Records. In a constant search for new talents, the owner recognized the potential of the band right away.

The Ramones signed their first contract to record an album. They stopped performing so they could lock themselves in the studio. They toiled over each song, and after two exhausting weeks, the album was finished.

The first album went on sale in record stores across the United States, and the cover image said it all: four guys with shaggy hair and serious faces. No frills, no bells or whistles. The Ramones were the reality they lived.

After the release of their first album, the band climbed onto a plane and headed off to London. They crossed the Atlantic and entered the English capital ready to perform. Young people lined up at the legendary concert venue, the Roundhouse, to attend the Ramones' first concert in Europe.

The concert was sold out. Even members of English punk bands who had come to see the Ramones perform were turned away at the door—although it's said that they were soon invited backstage by the Ramones themselves.

As Tommy yelled "1, 2, 3, 4!" and the band started playing, the Roundhouse exploded with emotion, and punk flooded the city.

The band established themselves as punk role models, inspiring their fans and English bands with the strength of their sound. From that day on, the Ramones would be remembered eternally as pioneers and leaders of punk rock.

RAMONES STUDIO ALBUMS

1,2,3,4!

HEY! HO!

- 🎵 RAMONES (1976)
- 🎵 LEAVE HOME (1977)
- 🎵 ROCKET TO RUSSIA (1977)
- 🎵 ROAD TO RUIN (1978)
- 🎵 END OF THE CENTURY (1980)
- 🎵 PLEASANT DREAMS (1981)
- 🎵 SUBTERRANEAN JUNGLE (1983)

- TOO TOUGH TO DIE (1984)

- ANIMAL BOY (1986)

- HALFWAY TO SANITY (1987)

- BRAIN DRAIN (1989)

- MONDO BIZARRO (1992)

- ACID EATERS (1993)

- ¡ADIOS AMIGOS! (1995)

LET'S GO!

LEARN MORE ABOUT THE HISTORY OF MUSIC WITH THESE GREAT BOOKS.

The origin of the band that conquered the world with electronic music.

The origin of one of the most ambitious and theatrical rock bands.

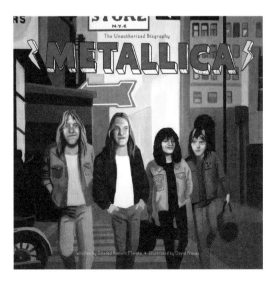

The electrifying adventure of the band that challenged metal's limits.

Follow this link to listen to the Ramones' first LP on Spotify

First published in the United States in 2020 by Sourcebooks

Text © 2018, 2020 Soledad Romero Mariño
Illustrations © 2018, 2020 Joe Padilla
Other art © mactovector_official/Freepik, kjpargeter/Freepik, FrankRamspott/Getty Images, mightyisland/Getty Images, allnickart//Getty Images, vecteezy.com
Cover and internal design © 2020 by Sourcebooks
Cover design by Brittany Vibbert/Sourcebooks
Internal design by Will Riley

Published by Sourcebooks eXplore, an imprint of Sourcebooks Kids
P.O. Box 4410, Naperville, Illinois 60567–4410
(630) 961-3900
sourcebookskids.com

Originally published as Band Records: *Ramones* in 2018 by Reservoir Kids, an imprint of Penguin Random House Grupo Editorial.

Library of Congress Cataloging-in-Publication Data is on file with the publisher.

Source of Production: PrintPlus Limited, Shenzhen, Guangdong Province, China
Date of Production: June 2020
Run Number: 5018898

Printed and bound in China.
PP 10 9 8 7 6 5 4 3 2 1

HEY! HO! LET'S GO!

SIDE A

1. Blitzkrieg Bop
2. Beat on the Brat
3. Judy I s a Punk
4. I Wanna Be Your Boyfriend
5. Chain Saw
6. Now I Wanna Sniff Some Glue
7. I Don't Wanna Go Down
   to the Basement